Acknowledgments

Grateful acknowledgment is given to the following journals, newspapers and anthologies in which some of these poems previously appeared:

Ad Hoc Monadnock (anthology)
The American Bard
Appalachia
Beloit Poetry Journal
The Christian Science Monitor
Field
Heartbeat of New England (anthology)
The Herald Tribune
The New York Times
Radcliffe Quarterly
The Uncommon Reader
The Worcester Review

"Bai Iordan Goes to the Opera" won the Erika Mumford Prize from The New England Poetry Club.

Viewpoint

Viewpoint

Juli Nunlist

HOBBLEBUSH BOOKS

ISBN-13: 978-0-9760896-3-6
ISBN-10: 0-9760896-3-7
Library of Congress Control Number: 2005938685

Composed at Hobblebush Books,
Brookline, New Hampshire

Printed in the United States of America

Text and titles are composed in Bembo, a serene face of true Renaissance structure produced by Monotype in 1929, based on a roman cut at Venice by Francisco Griffo in 1495.

Front cover painting by Marshall Nunlist
Back cover photograph by Janet Sidor

Published by:

Hobblebush Books

17-A Old Milford Road
Brookline, New Hampshire 03033

www.hobblebush.com

Just
Understand
Love
Is

Never
(Understand:
Never)
Lost
Is
Still
There

Juli Nunlist

Contents

IV

Foreword

IF THIS BOOK were a fairytale, each poem in *Viewpoint* would
be a white stone leading us through a seventy-five year journey,
and if we were incredibly fortunate, Juli would be with us, her
flannel shirt flapping, her eyes darting from stone to tree to
each of our faces. She would be talking, of course — not about
teaching music to dancers or composing music, or even about
her poetry — but about our work, about how to choose the best
words and place them in the best order, about how to listen, how
to hear. She would suggest looking from a different perspective,
using a different tense or voice. Above all, she would say to trust
the organic integrity of the poem in form and structure and, eyes
twinkling, would tell us to "lie to make the poem true." She is
the best of mentors, is relentless in her devotion to the work, and
inspires us to be the same.

Juli writes what needs to be written; she doesn't flinch when
facing loss, makes no excuses for her mistakes, observes and points
out what cannot be saved — the albino deer, the last dusky seaside
sparrow. She writes to understand. Her craft is impeccable.
No word, no space, no line is unexamined. Her life, too, has
undergone deep scrutiny and through her poetry — precise,
personal, and sometimes painful — we become part of her world,
which is our world as well.

For almost twenty-five years, Juli has been Susan Roney-O'Brien's beloved friend and most trusted critic. But it didn't take others that long to understand her immense talent and generosity. Juli ran a writers' workshop in Princeton, Massachusetts for twenty years. When she moved to Lebanon, New Hampshire five years ago, some of the participants, including Joan Erickson, Linda Warren and Susan continued to meet with her in her new home. Dorothy Anderson, who had met Juli at The Frost Place in Franconia, New Hampshire also joined us and brought Patricia (Pat) Fargnoli into the workshop. One thing became clear; Juli's work needed to be collected and published. Pat and I decided to do just that with the support of Juli's son Mark and that of the other poets in our group.

To put *Viewpoint* together, we sifted through over two hundred poems, choosing the ones we felt we couldn't leave out, then, in shaping the book, had to delete even some poems we both loved. We met, read poems, made choices and lists and examined many drafts, and ordered and re-ordered the manuscript. We hope what we have put together is not only a tribute to an astonishing person, but also a book of great worth that mirrors Juli's talent, generosity and craft. We offer our humble hope that you will open yourself to her words. The stones are gleaming. The poems are waiting.

November 20, 2005
Susan Roney-O'Brien and Patricia Fargnoli, Editors

Viewpoint

I

Directions

In a field lie flat
on your stomach. Press into
the earth beneath you.
Push through to China.
Feel the whole
length of your body
weighted against
hard earth,
stalk and stubble.
Cheek scored,
scarred with stem lines,
lie loose,
lie heavy,
rolling through space
on top of the world.

Turn over.
Flat on your back
grab a root,
tuft of grass.
Look *down* at the sky.
Clutch tight:
earth's *above* you,
tugging to loosen
the grip of your fingers,
to spin off without you.
Hang on
with both fists,
dig heels in
hard, hard.
Cling for life
to the underside
of the planet, awaiting

the terrible moment
of letting go,
the terrible wonder
of falling, falling,
falling into the sky.

Discovery Made While Adjusting
the Bindings on My Snowshoes

The sky today is what is meant
by the word blue, the words clear,
cold, winter and deep.

Everything else — black bole of tree,
red barn, white snow, white house —
is holding its breath,

keeping quite still
so the whole world can hear
the silent triumphant shout of the sky:

blue

Skyscape with Birds
for My Small Daughter

Your eyebrows
are wings
I watch mood migrations

As for your hair
I do not understand why nature
makes no use of brown
for a cloud color

When you laugh
I hear juncos
Their down forms your cheek

Cloud   wing
and the light air of a feather of laughter

Journey

He drifts in and out of sleep.
The *Book of Birds* has slipped to the floor beside him
and a flamingo rises,
neck outstretched, legs trailing, wings beating in silence.
The room has become a lagoon, the bird wades in the shallows,
stirring up mollusks with the sieve of its bill.

Now he awakens in Madagascar,
on the Ridge of Ancona, a summit
nine thousand four hundred thirty-six feet in height.
Far below on the shore flamingos by hundreds, thousands,
are flocking to join the bird who brought him here.
He tastes the names of the trees of Tsaratanana:
ebony, rosewood, sandalwood, palm,
bamboo, the traveler's tree.
Lemurs surround him, watch him, staring dull-eyed.
He counts the rings on the tails of those that cling
to the rocks nearby,
and notes the fat stored in the rumps of others.

At midnight he rises,
prepares for the ritual purification of hands:
the chanting of invocations, the tossing of beans.

He has found the land called Lemuria, lost by the mapmakers.

Amateur Astronomer

for M.B.N.

He stands upon the earth that spins
and makes a mirror for the skies
to channel starlight to his eyes.
The finished product he designed
will take a year or more to grind,
at least one orbit of the earth
before his lens is brought to birth:
the stars will wait. So he begins,
a quiet smile on his lips,
a universe at his fingertips.

Barriers

My neighbor burns the underbrush each year
That separates his own north field from mine.
He says he thinks but one dividing line
Of youngling maples is enough. But he
Forgets the staying power of any vine,
And long before November days are here
A thick dark tangle's creeping toward each tree,
As if to prove more barriers between
Two men than just one slender line of green.

Lament for a Potter

*for Theodore Randall, dying of a
brain tumor called a "butterfly"*

I look at your small gray bowl
on my kitchen counter, and the blue ashtray
shaped like a leaf,
and see your fingers curved on the moist clay
forming pots, urns, pitchers, useful
objects to pour from, plant in, hold things.
I think of a life of teaching, molding,
trying, you said, *not for the pot never seen before,
but for the pot that recalls
all pottery.*

Now the gray bowl of your head against the pillow
holds fragments of thought like bits of dried-up clay,
a shadow thrown by this strange last
winged shape your brain conceived.
Silent, the potter's wheel waits for your hands
to coax inchoate stuffs into fresh forms,
sculpted expressions of an art of living.
But you are being turned, yourself, on a different lathe.

Storm

Who were we, and what were we doing there?
It was not a night for men to be out: the trees
Shivered and tossed in the wind, and the wind grew bold
And threatened to drive us in if we wouldn't go in.
Better for us to go. It was not our world.
Sometime during the night the planet changed hands.
We were no longer masters (or even allowed
To think we were masters). Nothing was left to choice.
And so we went in, but even there we could hear
The wind's wild clamoring voice.

The house door rattled, and something beat at the blind.

Even a farmhouse can't be depended upon.
For what in the world to a wind is wood or stone
But something to bend and split, to crash and roll?

(And the thin pale flesh that houses the thin pale soul —
When was it ever a house to keep out death?)

There was nothing for us to do but take our chance
With everything else that owned to a little breath,
And stay inside and pretend there was nothing amiss.
For this was the night of the year the wind and ice
Reclaimed the planet, pronounced it theirs once more.
And man had better be in and bolt the door.

For Mark

who caught a toad while apple-gathering,
blue-green and small, pulsing with silent frightened life,
eyes bulging, staring
(cupped in his hands he brought it, caring,
wanting a box,
a piece of screen, a pan of water,
rocks and moss,
dead flies for food)

in the cool orchard dark
melodious trill spurts from the beating throat sac
spilling green song over dew-wet grasses,
filling the night with hint of drenching shower,
willing the hour of rain
for leaf and flower

though I know the murmurous sound of the peepers at night
will never be less for the loss of one
toad in a brown box squatting,
waiting, a warty lump of fear,
abrupt resolution of the Now of a toad and the Here,
cadence of green song, ultimate breath —

for Mark, who caught a toad while apple-gathering,
tears for a toad's death.

Spring Snow

Here comes the first bird
with the first half-light.
What will he say when he finds
a world of white?
He left it turning yellow-green
last night.

What if he hurries
back to the apple-bough
to tell the rest:
There's been some strange mistake,
forget the nest.

What if they gather
in the morning dark
a question to debate:
if by some stretch of feather
they've overshot the mark?

One of them says that he
is sure he remembers
a barn and a certain tree
from the last two Novembers.

Most of them clearly know
spring is a settled thing.
One light belated snow
(at least if they're worth a wing)
oughtn't to make them go.

Albino Deer

She came at dusk
to the water's edge,
down to the dam.

The sky over Hunlock Creek
hung bleak with a burden of snow,
leaving wood and water black.

She could not know
the savage trick
Nature had played on her,

making her strange pale beauty
a high relief against
the utmost black of pine and fir.

The hunter knew his luck:
under the sky's held breath
death came to the white doe.

The silent snow now drifting
can do no more than blur
this wild red pattern.

Viewpoint

If you look
this way and that
you will see things

differently. This way
you see the fisherman
in the blue cap

is holding a net,
in fact he is
mending it,

retying a knot
that has come undone
at one corner.

You imagine the net tonight
filled with the silver gleam
of fish scales

as his boat bumps
against the dock, its deck
luminous with his catch.

But if you look that way,
you see the fisherman is holding
an enormous number

of holes tied together
with string,
and he is trying,

by knotting the corner,
to keep one of the holes
from escaping.

II

The Bear's Favor

When Mrs. Cirulis
washes our kitchen floor
she chooses Chopin.
Mazurkas, waltzes, she says,
nocturnes not good,
for scrubbing not good —
dreaming, slow.
I put on a stack of records:
Brahms Intermezzi
for living room — she
prefers Sviatoslav Richter,
though he is Russian.
He can't help, she says,
he was born.
A symphony by Sibelius
for bathrooms — *Over*
the water running
I hear, she explains.

When Mrs. Cirulis
walked out of Latvia
after the war,
she took with her three
things: the clothes she had on,
a sack of potatoes, and
her youngest son — he was ten.
My husband was artist-painter,
she says, *he was famous,*
they killed him. My oldest son
also they killed.
The middle one —
Mrs. Cirulis shrugs —
he stayed. He became
one of them. He chose.

From Ludva they walked across Latvia
to a barren spot on the shore
beyond Pavilotsa.
Many nights, she recalls,
and the rivers to cross.
Never in day.
She has not explained
how they found a boat, has no words
for the Baltic Sea journey,
the years in a German
refugee camp. *We are here,*
she says, *that is all.*
My son learns the law
in college. I scrub to make so.

Mrs. Cirulis comes
every Thursday, and every
Thursday forgets: she brings
down two flights of stairs
the pillowcase full of sheets
for the laundry man.
I laugh. *Not yet,* I remind her,
there's shirts to go in.
She chuckles. *I did you again*
a bear's favor, she says,
something I do for you good
and is not for you good
but is trouble. She pauses.
Like Russians, she says,
they come into my country,
they do for my country
the bear's favor, yes?

Four Jatovsky Songs

Nina

to her piano lesson comes
(a pig-tailed poem in pale blue smocking)
up the dark stair

one fist of roses (pink) for Mr. Jatovsky
in the other dog-eared Bach
a brook of song

O small blue poem of roses
on your way
to be set to music

2

Stephen Looks at Naomi, His Daughter

My delight has taken her sorrow to the garden,
buried her anger like a bone among tulip bulbs,
finding a dark comfort in the dirt.

At two she has discovered that earth has a way with grief.

3

Lyuba, My Sister

Lyuba is gone
and Anna sits remembering.
Someone has opened a door and closed a door.

Lyuba is gone
and Anna hears a voice
(Anna! Anna!)
from the other side of a looking-glass of years.

What did we say when we were last together?
Was it something to serve as a

    farewell
Lyuba, my sister?

4
An Expression of Pity for the People
Who Live in Appletree Lane

(for David Jatovsky)

In the morning
on my way to you
I pass by Appletree Lane.

A yellow leaf is falling,
but the sun is warm on the houses,
and a boy skips down the road
singing to himself,
pauses
to make a cat's cradle.

He is happy.
All of Appletree Lane is bright and cheerful.

But how this can be, I do not know:
for who in Appletree Lane is on his way to you?

January Thaw

Eddie
      in red wool cap
          and bright blue anorak

painstaking
      deliberate
          (*andante*)

trundling
      a wheelbarrow full of logs
          from the spot

where the rowan tree
      had fallen
          to the place back of the barn

where we stack
      our winter wood
          then trundling

the empty barrow
      back for another load
          pausing now and then

to stare
      across the field
          toward the house

where this morning
      something
          let go

loosed him
      from his secret
          world

(I saw it
           from the kitchen window)
              and set him

hopping
        (*allegro*)
                with a gleeful smile

from one foot to the other
        Eddie
                dancing on the duckboards

The Parlor

Through a beaded curtain
the child steps, wary,
into the darkened room.
She is seven —
alone, eager,
and fearful.
She is not supposed
to be here.

From a heavy oval gilt frame
on the wall facing her
that other child
gives back her solemn stare:
Elizabeth — dead at seven,
of diphtheria.
Silence, trembling,
fills the room.

The shepherd and shepherdess,
patient on the top shelf
of the forbidden cabinet,
await the longed-for rendezvous.
There is a key in the cabinet door.
The child turns it.
The door creaks open.
The dead Elizabeth watches.

O treasured moment!
to cup in the hands
small porcelain people.

The grownups are upstairs,
gathered around Great-aunt Minnie's bed.
The child knows
that Great-aunt Minnie is sick
and not sick.

She has heard them talking:
something about the dead Elizabeth's
dying, long ago.

A glance, quick flicker
at the portrait —
then back to the cabinet.
Here are a tiny jade hippopotamus,
a green glass toad,
an ivory giraffe:
the dead Elizabeth's
private jungle.

A step in the hall.
The child shrinks,
shivers into shadow.
O let him not
be coming to look for her —
Great-uncle Ozzie,
with his bony lap and hands
and his wet kisses.

The Peahen Observes Her Lord

Cock of the palace dunghill
pacing the lawn,
strut your utmost, quiver.

Courting adulation
spread that lacy fan
of feather-velvet.

Ringed with blue and bronze
each iridescent eye
glares its pride of power.

You dance, or think you dance,
approaching your dun possessions:
squat brown harem hens.

Elevate your ego,
rattle quills and scream
raucous as a crow.

Bring the splendor forward
enveloping your body,
leaving your ass exposed.

When I Think of Legs

I think of Marilyn,
the fat blonde teller
in the bank on Quincy Street,
whose right leg had to be amputated.
The staff at the bank
took up a collection
to help her pay
for an artificial limb.

When her mother brought Marilyn
down in a wheelchair
so she could thank everybody,
she said the toughest part
of the whole business
was trying to make up her mind
what kind to get: a leg
that matched the one she had left,
or the kind of leg—elegant, slender—
she'd always wanted.

Unfinished

                              the kid in sneakers
running home to a whistle past thick hedges in the summer dusk,
leaving shrill cries of allee-allee-in-free from the Flanagans' front
yard — the one who flew to the moon with Joe in orange crates,
who found the gray goose feather and believed it was the key to
a door somewhere leading to someplace special on no map of
the world that was — the awkward, spotty-faced wallflower, hands
and feet too big, sitting tense, eyes on the floor the first Friday
evening at Peter Paul Pearce's dancing school, waiting not to be
asked, not to be noticed, not to be there — the unwanted one,
street-angel, house-devil, hating her self and her body, twisted up in
the cold leather Morris chair with books and a quart of coffee ice
cream, wanting the world to go by, disappear, not happen

Harriet (c. 1926)

We knew she'd fallen
face down in a fire
when she was very small.
At least that's what they said.
We didn't talk about it much.
But she had no face,
no real face like ours,
instead thick lumps of raw pink flesh,
seamed with scars
as if they'd been stitched together,
her nose a ragged flap of skin
held by a *safety pin*
to what should have been a cheek,
eyes like raisins deep in lard.

We used to walk to school
in a bunch — Gus Vanderhof,
Joe Flanagan and I,
Sissy Hoagland, her kid brother Calvin,
and Harriet.
Harriet was smaller.
She scuffed along behind
trying to catch up,
never said *Wait for me,*
never said anything.
How old were we?
six? seven? ten? Those years
just knowing she was there,
knowing it was Harriet,
we felt a kind of dark discomfort,
a formless, heavy anger,
fear.

Why did it happen?
Why did we have to make it worse,
not letting her catch up?

1924

Millicent Davis lived upstairs,
Millicent Davis, pale of skin,
dark of hair, with eyes like buttons.

Millicent was a perfect child.
I know: my mother told me so,
and so did Millicent.

Her hair was always combed and curled,
her dresses neat. My skirts were torn,
I chopped my hair with pinking shears.

One afternoon in every week
her mother came to tea with mine,
bringing Millicent, of course,

and Millicent's favorite china doll.
They came downstairs in their Sunday best,
Millicent's mother wearing a hat.

The china doll was bibbed in white.
Millicent carried a handkerchief
and sipped her tea and was polite.

Millicent was the teacher's pet.
Millicent was *good*. She knew
the answer to every question asked.

Everything that Millicent said
was gospel truth. I lied a lot,
and wished that Millicent was dead —
and knew that I would roast in hell.

Archytas of Tarentum, Scientist,
5th Century B.C., to His Son

I cannot give you the bird itself,
nor would I if I could.
Take this instead. I have tried to match
shape and color — though this must be larger,
with angled wings and a notched tail.
Well, not true wings, you must imagine them:
the papyrus stretched — so — over a reed frame.
The bits of material knotted into this cord
provide balance. Be not rough in your handling:
it is light and fragile.
                Oh yes, it will fly.
Not as the bird, but the wind will make it dip
and glide, soar and swoop. It will have
its own grace. You will see. Here, let me loop
the cord around your finger.
                    Pull it behind you,
look over your shoulder, watch it rise.
I have named it for the smallest unit of weight
of the Pharaoh Amenophthis of Egypt. I call it *kite*.
                        Now run —

The surface of the moon

is a sublime desolation,
wrote Fred L. Whipple
in *Earth, Moon and Planets*,
The Blakiston Company, 1941.

Wrong, Fred, wrong.
Unless you are dead, Fred, come flying now
to the rescue of the barren lunar plains
and rugged lunar mountains you describe so lovingly.

Moon evil is abroad, Fred, sublimity will be destroyed, Fred,
by Celestis, Inc., of Houston, Texas,
which is now taking reservations for the first lunar burials
to be launched in the fall of 2001.

A modest $125 K, and a four-day flight of 240,000 miles
with instant interment upon collision
will guarantee an eternity of peace and quiet.

No need to pay for perpetual care, Fred,
the nature of the universe determines that.

Celestis, says co-founder Charlie Chafey,
aims to open the space frontier for everyone —
though they may be too late for you, Fred.

First launch may be delayed a bit
if Disney and Time Warner both
should claim first dibs for landing space
in the Sea of Tranquility.

O Moon of myth and mystery, master of ocean tides
and legendary friend of lovers, call now, *call now*
for Fred L. Whipple, who said, in his cosmic innocence,
Nothing ever happens on the moon.

My friend Luiz Moran

tells of his father's village
in the mountains of Peru:
every man a grower of grapes
and a maker of wine.

After the harvest
when the wine is made,
Señor Moran with a bottle of his best
visits the house of a neighbor.

With you, sir —
each samples the other's wine.
(Who in the village
will have the season's finest?)

The neighbor and Señor Moran
visit the house of another neighbor
— and so on for a pleasant afternoon and evening
With you, sir —

and the whole village
is sleeping early.

How the Hermit
Came to Church

Old Doc Loomis
it was who asked
if any had seen
the hermit's lantern
since the night of the blizzard,
but none could recall
the last there'd been
that flicker of light
in the old man's window —
uncertain star
on Mount Wachusett.

The room grew still.
(Christmas Eve,
and the whole town gathered
for Christ Church supper
and midnight service.)
Eyes questioned eyes,
heads were shaken,
soup spoons lowered.
My god, someone said,
he's gone, then, alone.
He's up there dead,
another muttered,
like as not frozen.
The voices rose:
Poor old man!
We can't be sure —
How'll we get him?
What'll we do?
The ground's too hard,
have to wait some time.
For the January thaw?
Most like till spring.

But it's Christmas Eve —
we can't just leave him,
said Biddy Northrop,
folding her apron.
The only way
to bring him down
is for Barney Coleman
to take his sleigh,
those two great Clydes
and a couple of men.
She looked at Barney.
He grinned and nodded.
Who's going with me?

Five hours later
they heard the bells,
(Barney'd forgotten
to take them off)
the sleigh bells ringing
down the mountain,
clear on the Christmas
midnight air —
giving the hermit
a joyful ride,
ringing him in
to the Christ Church service
for the first and the last time.
Rosy with wine
the townsfolk gathered
to make him welcome,
greeting the sleigh
with a rousing cheer —
for Barney, the men
and the horses, and for
the hermit himself,
who, in life apart,
in death made merry
with other men.

The Butcher

We watched him cut five pork chops
and place them with care in a row
on thick white paper.

The shop was small and sunlit,
its walls a gleaming white.
Sawdust covered the floor.

The butcher-block, heavy, square,
stood next to a counter
holding scales.

We watched him pause to choose
from a blue bowl filled with water
sprigs of fresh parsley

to dress the pink meat. His hands,
big and clean, and red from washing and washing,
were gentle.

He wrapped the green-decked chops
in a neat package for us. I said:
You are an artist, Mr. Lohman,

and he nodded, smiling, and said:
Well, you know how it is
when you love your work.

Bai Iordan Goes to the Opera

(Bai Iordan rolls on the ground, shaking with laughter:

> About me she wrote a poem
> in New York, he crows,
>
> listen, everybody!)

For many weeks
Bai Iordan, herdsman of the village of Pordim,
has carefully saved his leva.
Three times he has gone hungry
in order that the leva might increase.

Today at last he is going to Sofia, a journey of five hours on the train,
to the national opera.

There are not enough leva
for Kaka Mitka, his slim and jolly wife,
to accompany him.
But she does not mind.
(It is good that Iordan is going to Sofia, Kaka Mitka says,
for he will return singing.
In the days to come he will sing *Carmen, Thais, Boris Godunov* —
of course he will sing in Bulgarian.

He will bring *Carmen* to Pordim —
to Kaka Mitka, to the village, to the cows and horses!)

He sets forth now in his only suit
of rough brown wool.

At the opera house (this makes Bai Iordan smile, when later he tells us)
the ladies on either side of him will draw away
in elegant disgust at his smell.

(The barn is in your clothes,
says Kaka Mitka, laughing.)

But the song is in your heart,
O Bai Iordan,
herdsman of the village of Pordim.

Noah's Wife, on the Third Day

What are we going to do with all that excrement?
Not to worry about mosquitoes and such like,
but think of the elephants! *Ham! Shem! Japheth!*
Did any of you remember to bring shovels?
Your father has had enough on his mind,
he can't be expected to think of everything.
The girls are all right, though they need to be told
what to do, like daughters-in-law the world over.
At least they do what they're told.
But Ham — he's utterly worthless, seasick
the whole time. And I don't like the way those pythons
are eyeing the sheep and goats. I've told them:
One squeeze and you go out that window.
I'm certain the good Lord didn't intend
there to be any savagery in His brave new world.

III

If only I

had done (said?)
this, that, or the other thing,
whatever it was—
or not done it (not said it
in that particular way?)

maybe the sun would be rising in the west,
giraffes singing like larks,
the word *rage* have only one meaning:
a current fad.

The day

Mr. Aristides came
to take my mother
to the nursing home—
I needn't have worried.

He rolled up the drive
in a huge black
limousine. Three ladies
in elegant dresses,
gloved and hatted,
accompanied him.

They entered the house
through the kitchen door
as if they were gracing
a palace. All four
gave me pleasant smiles
as they hurried by
on their way upstairs
to my mother's room.

Mr. Aristides said:
Good day, Mrs. Moora,
swept Lillie May
up in his arms
and trotted downstairs.
The ladies followed.
Two carried suitcases,
the other, the walker.

Mr. Aristides, smiling
and cheerful,
settled Lillie May
in the passenger seat.
The elegant ladies

got in the back
and the black limousine
hummed away down the drive.

I stood and watched,
waiting to wave
goodbye to Lillie May.
She didn't look back.

I Like to Think of You, Lillie May

for my mother

Today I gave your blue flannel nightgown
to young Cindy Listovitch.
Cleaning cupboards we found it
bunched up among the afghans
you crocheted for me.

White cotton eyelet frames a yoke,
tiny forget-me-nots dot the pale blue.
I like to think of you, Lillie May,
in that nightgown.
At night you never had tantrums.

Afternoons when I came home from work
you'd screech obscenities,
fling books and dishes, yell:
You treat me like an animal,
you're a devil, not a daughter.

But at night when I undressed you,
turned down the bed and tucked you in,
you'd grasp my arm and whisper:
You know I didn't mean it,
don't you, Elizabeth?

One summer day a neighbor
heard you screaming, called the police.
I knew our home could no longer hold you,
but not how to tell you this.
I underrated you, Lillie May.

I'd lifted you out of the bathtub onto a chair,
was on my knees drying your feet—
you took my face between gnarled hands and said:

You are an angel, but you cannot live
like this. You must put me from you now.

You had to wait seven years
in the nursing home.
                                        This morning
I gave your blue flannel nightgown
to Cindy Listovitch. She helps me sort things out.
She wishes I'd been her mother.

Homeward Bound from
Sunset View Nursing Home

There is no God.
I have been to see my mother.
There is no mercy.
I have been to see my mother.
There is no life.
I have been to see my mother.
There is no death.
I have been to see my mother.
There is no mother.

The Way It Was

When he stuck his head
out the trolley-car window
a passing truck bashed Uncle George
in the forehead, giving him
one permanently raised eyebrow.

With his thick black hair, fierce
black eyes, and that single
black wing soaring to his temple,
Uncle George looked like the Devil.
Believe me, his nine kids *behaved.*

So did Aunt Bertha. Across sixty years
I hear my mother's voice reporting to Dad—
She sat on the edge of the bed
sobbing: Oh Lil, Lil,
I'm pregnant again.

Thoughts Relative to a Visit, Castle Nursing Home

Uncle Louis
chose a gun,
spread his brains all over the living room
for his son
to discover.

Stepmother Hazel
selected Seconal.
It took her breath away.

Brother Bob tried
carbon monoxide
four times. It exhausted him.

(Daughter Kate
considered broken glass,
but came to no
conclusion.)

Mother Moora,
on the other hand,
had a stroke of luck:
spent seven years
in her very own vegetable garden
without knowing it.

Insurance

Each night before
going to bed
Great-aunt Lucy,
at ninety-three,
sets out a clean
cereal bowl,
cup and saucer,
places a fresh
linen napkin
in the walnut
ring Great-uncle
Ned carved for her.
That way, she says,
she can be sure
of waking up
in the morning.
How can you die
when your breakfast
things are waiting?

The bells

are ringing. It is Christmas Eve
and you are making your first moves
toward getting born.
A Brooklyn cabbie picks us up—
your father, me, you—from in front
of a small house
on New York Avenue, to drive
over the great bridge whose builder,
Roebling, your own
great-grandfather taught. Far uptown
Manhattan's Woman's Hospital
waits your coming.
I am in pain and frightened, but
your father grips my hand in his,
and the cabbie
says: *Don't worry, Ma'am, we'll make it,*
just you listen to them bells—they're
ringin' for us.
He's right: the carillons of all
Manhattan's churches giving voice
to welcome you
into our world. The midnight air,
filled with the sound of chimes, magics
the battered cab
into a winged sleigh, and you,
from your deep dreamless sleep, are rung
into being.

Lie Deep

How does a seed
withhold its need
under the earth,
waiting to come
to a spring birth?

How does it keep
patience beneath
cover so deep,
frozen and numb?
How does it know
when it may breathe,
when it may bleed?

Let it be now
covered with snow.
Let it lie deep
in a white sleep.

Koolo the Cat the Black One

Christopher, Kate, and Michael
in a row on the bench in the kitchen
eating lunch—
pattern of round brown eyes and yellow hair,
mouthfuls of words with interruptions of soup spoons,
now a pause

a solemn sucking of milk through colored straws.

Christopher says:
Koolo the cat the black one—
Goes alone to the wood, says Kate—
Walks alone, says Michael,
and sometimes he never comes home for breakfast,
says Michael.

Maybe Koolo catches mice, I tell them,
and isn't hungry.

How,
says Christopher,
do cats know
that mice taste good?
(alone to the wood, alone to the wood, sings Kate)

Instinct, I tell them,
and at their puzzled look I add:
built-in,
comes-with-the-cat,
they know, they know.

For thousands of years, I tell them, oh
for thousands of years cats have eaten mice.
Ever since there were cats and mice.

But that's not very nice of cats, says Kate,
Too late for change, says Michael.

How,
says Christopher,
did the first cat know
that the first mouse would taste good? How?
says Michael.
(alone in the wood, alone in the wood, sings Kate).

Letter to my daughter Kate

(to be included with a certified check
for $67.43, signed: Pollyanna Pig)

from among the shards of pale blue porcelain
and the scattering of bills and coins
the ghost of Pollyanna Pig says
hi, here is your half

there were several Indian-head nickels
and one 1887 nickel
(your grandmother would have been one year old)
and an IOU from Mark
for seventy-five cents
and six dollars in pennies
(that's twenty-four towers of twenty-five each)

> *in the end I think love, if it be love*
> *rejects the big things: declarations*
> *betrayals*
> *tragic errors and confrontations*
> *and remembers*
> *only the little things*
> *such as that under her chin*
> *was the softest spot in the world, and that*
> *her eyebrows spoke a language known only to*
> *birds*

the year's first pussy willows
are on sale now at Heinen's
and today Mark flew your old red dragon kite, and we
wish you were here

All my lost daughters . . . December 25, 1981

First daughter
sturdy elf
perhaps you returned to the Santa who brought you

Second daughter
bumble-bee
your buzzing dance led you to a great hospital hive

Third daughter
solemn wax doll
the nineteenth case in medical history bears your name

Fourth daughter
broken-jawed toothless waif
only the inner scars remain

Fifth daughter
many-faced Eve
all the world might have been your stage

Sixth daughter
witch-woman
you doubled your troubles with a poison brew

Seventh daughter
a stranger named Kate
the woman all my daughters have become

The Storm Coat

It is cold, fourteen above,
a light wind blowing spirals
of dry snow. I slip my arms
into the sleeves of your coat—
the old mud-colored storm coat
you wore in college, with its
soft, rough, ersatz fur collar
and lining of red flannel.
I've kept it for eighteen years,
each time we moved hung it up
in a new closet, never
before put it on. But now
I'm going out for the mail—
and you are coming with me
whether or not you want to.

Across the road the mailbox
on its white post promises
nothing. Oh, maybe a bill
or two and the usual
junk mail.
          There will be nothing
from you, though I wrote once more
this Christmas, your fortieth
birthday—I suppose I should
know better by this time, but
that old saw about hope is
uncomfortably true.
                        Well,
I was wrong about the mail:
today the box is empty—
no bills, no sweepstakes come-on.

I cross the road again, hands
thrust deep into your pockets.
There's a bit of paper crushed

in one and I pull it out.
Straightening it, through a blur
of drifting snowflakes I read:
Mother, I may be a bitch
but I love you. Me.
                    Walking
back to the house with it clutched
in one hand, I wrap my arms
about myself, hugging me
with the sleeves of your storm coat.

Cat's Cradle

It was a puzzle, wasn't it—
how we transferred those first simple shapes
from my hands to yours and back,
and back again, each time the delicate
architecture of string becoming
more complicated, further and further
from the original.

It was meant to be a game, wasn't it—
with each of us trying in turn
to create a more intricate pattern,
our fingers careful never to touch
each other's, but to master
the precarious art of avoidance
while building those fragile
relationships of angle and tension,
till all of a sudden one of us
slipped, and the whole thing collapsed,
falling inward, leaving us
with ruin on our hands.

Strangers

A tall thin woman in black
carrying a white parasol
walks through city streets
looking for a shop where she can sell
a few pieces of old jewelry.
I do not know her,
have never seen her before.
When she finds the shop I discover
I do not know the jeweler.
The street mob outside the doors
of the old mansion where
all of a sudden I find myself
shouts, shouts to come in.
From a window I search
the many screaming faces.
Not one is familiar.

But once in a dream
I knew everybody—well,
there were only two people:
you and me. I was walking down
West 84th Street on the south side,
downhill toward the river,
and you were across the street,
walking up the north side toward Broadway.
It was raining a little,
and the street, buildings, sidewalks,
the few trees were all grey,
the lampposts black. The river lay
like a thick grey snake—
I could see right through the park.
I was grey too: hair, face, hands,
clothing, but you wore earth-colors:
oak red and honey and brown. I watched you
as we passed, the street between us,

and wanted to call out to you
but my voice stuck in my throat.
You did not look my way,
though you knew I was there.

Last Glimpse of a Daughter,
Monday Morning, March 24th, 1975

It was raining a little.
You leaned out of the window
of your fourth floor walk-up, long
brown hair blowing. A chill breeze
stirred the curtain behind you.
A single geranium
perched precariously on
the sill beside your elbows.
You waved. I waved, unfolded
the old umbrella you had
given me and walked on up
West 84th Street, looking
back from moment to moment
to wave again. You waved too,
each time I looked. Each time I
looked you were smaller, of course.
I crossed West End Avenue
and went on up to Broadway
where the bus would stop, the one
to take me to the downtown
terminal where I would catch
the airport's black limousine.
I had to wait for some time:
all the wrong buses came by.
I kept looking back at you
and waving. You kept looking
up toward me, and I believe
you were still waving too, though
it was difficult to see
through rain and tears. Then the right
bus came, and I got on it
clumsily, wet umbrella
flapping close against my legs,
your bus token in my hand.
I looked once more. You were still
there. I've never seen you since.

Villanelle for Kate

I do not know how to say what I want to say.
Words no longer seem to have much meaning.
Listen. Try to hear. I must find a way.

In the beginning the words for you and me
were daughter and mother. Remember? In the beginning
I thought I knew how to say what I meant to say.

Even when you started to drift away,
I thought it was a natural process of weaning.
Listen. Try to hear. We must find a way

somehow to speak to one another, free
of old restraint. In the little time remaining
we must learn how to say what we need to say:

simple words—love, forgiving—that we
have forgotten to use. Is it too late for learning
to listen? Trying to hear? Is there no way

to reach you? To shout: Can't we see
the time is now? And now is not for mourning
what in the past I did not know how to say,
nor you to hear. Listen. Find a way.

Coping in the Big Apple

Last I heard
she'd been mugged three times:
once late at night in a subway tunnel—
four of them, one with a knife at her throat,
wanting her money and anything else she had,
watch, compact, ring—she gave it all and said
I've got a long walk home, how about a bus token?
They laughed and tossed her a couple.
The next one knocked her down and grabbed her purse,
got her so mad she chased him and grabbed it back,
socked him on the head with it.
The third was a big one, scary—
came into the vestibule of the old brownstone
just as she reached for the key to the inside door, said
*Take me upstairs with you, go on, open the door and take me
upstairs.* She looked him over, key in hand, and said
Fuck off, you goddamn bloody bastard, just fuck off.
He just fucked off. That's the last I heard.

South-winging Birds

As if some force impelled them all as one,
Some master bird-thought bidding them be gone,
I see a flock of thousands rise, and then
Forget to heed, and settle down again,
And rise and fall. A meadow seems to move,
Almost to breathe, a pulse-beat of dark feather.
How do they have it in them so together
Against the wind and cold southward to turn,
And northward come in season? Men might learn
Something from this going with the weather.

Marble Summer

The summer I was ten
was the marble summer.
Bought a bag at Woolworth's,
twelve for a dime—that shows
how long ago it was.
A string bag full of rust,
blood red, burgundy, cream—
only aggies, realies:
no blue-green glass for me.
Started with twelve: finished
with two thousand seven
hundred twenty-three. All
mine. No boy in town would
play with me by August.

Without Dad's permission
got a haircut like Bob's.
You can't put cut hair back.
Worth the grim displeasure
and a brother's jeering:
*Short hair won't do it. Pants
won't do it, dummy. You
can't do it: no equipment.
See?* Poking the damned thing
out for me to envy.

So how could I do it?
Will? Determination?
Perseverance and an
aching, empty longing
couldn't seem to do it.
Prayer had never done it.

But at the pony track
they knew I was a boy
and gave me the feisty ones.

I rode the wild ones, me,
while Helen and Louise
went plodding round and round
the ring with a modest
shiver of delight. I
knew ecstasy.
                    Of course
it couldn't last for long.
September came, and school,
and challis dresses, smocked—
Mom's patient, careful hands.
Marbles were put away.
It would be months before
I'd be a boy again.
And then at Christmas Aunt
Marie spoiled everything
with her gift: silk panties.
God. Silk panties. Always
before there had been books.
What gets into people?

So Bob was right. There was
no way it could be done,
be done for keeps, that is.

Still with pants and short hair,
sometimes I think: what if
the gods had said: *O.K.,*
let's give her what she wants.
Think what I would have missed:
Marshall and Kate and Mark,
all my real winnings,
my true deliverance from
the burden of the marble
summer of my boyhood.

I have just finished mending

your old blue sleeveless sweater:
the bottom was raveling
and there was a small moth hole
in the back. You've worn it for
seventeen years. I don't know
how many times it's needed
mending. I asked why on earth
you keep wearing the shabby
old thing. *Kate*, you said—so I
knew: it was our daughter's gift.
All right. I'll keep mending it.

IV

The Poem

Alberta Turner, in 50 Contemporary Poets:
*"A child may be rude but not impertinent
when he picks up your shoe and asks . . ."*

Whose is it?
    It's mine.
    And yours.
    It belongs to anyone who wants it
    and to many who will never see it
    or know it exists, or care.
    To Franny Holloway, a freshman at Swarthmore,
    dead fifty-four years.
    To the young woman ahead of me yesterday
    in the checkout line at the supermarket,
    whose beautiful autistic child looked at me and said:
    apricot, apricot.

What did you buy it for?
    To give away. (I paid for it a long time ago.)

Why is it black?
    Because black was the color of my typewriter ribbon
    —and my true love's hair (though now that is white)
    —and my song.

Where are the laces?
    I'm glad you ask.
    You're not meant to see them.
    They're what hold the parts together,
    loose but firm,
    a weaving of words.

Did you put the hole in the bottom?
    Yes.
    I wanted it to end without ending,

wanted a space in the air around it,
wanted it to go wherever it might take you.

May I try it on?
  Please do.
  That's what it's for.

Ode to the Bathtubs

i

He remembers
 the bathtub
  in the brothel at Emigrant Gap

(California, 1926),
 where he stayed
  while working on a hydro-electric dam.

Adjoining the bath
 was a room with a faro table
  and a barber's chair.

The brothel was built
 on stilts
  on the hillside—

water had to be lugged
 from the Merced River
  in buckets.

When he pulled the plug
 he could look
  through the plug hole,

watch soapy water
 plunge fifty feet
  to the ground,

cascade down
 the Sierra mountainside
  another thousand feet or more,

leaving a gray soapy stain,
 a rut of erosion
  on the high alpine slope.

ii
I remember
    the bathtub
        upstairs

in the two-family house
    on Brookfield Road
        (Montclair, New Jersey, 1928),

and me soaking,
    sobbing, soaking,
        trying to get clean again

knowing that ugly red stream
    would spurt forth
        not just this once,

but always from now on,
    next month, each month,
        every month.

iii
He remembers chasing the lizards
    from the wooden bathtub
        in the 200-year-old

high-raftered building
    at Coamo Springs (Puerto Rico, 1935),
        and the girl who would bring hot water

to add to the mineral spring,
    and stay, if he wished,
        to bathe him.

Later,
    he would climb back up
        to the little inn,

sit out under the jacaranda tree,
 wait for the servant to bring a daiquiri,
  watch wild monkeys swing back and forth.

 iv
I remember the Honeymoon Bathtub
 at Garland House
  (London, 1938):

eight feet long,
 a wall of mirror
  beside it.

I remember
 four feet
  in eight feet.

 v
We remember
 the dingy bathtub
  in the three-room apartment

on West 115th Street
 (New York City, 1940),
  where we first made acquaintance

with the permanent tenants: cockroaches,
 those ubiquitous
  seagulls of the sink.

 vi
We cannot forget
 the bathtub
  in the house with the willow tree

on Pioneer Avenue
    (Shavertown, Pennsylvania, 1947),
        where Kate's thin little sticks

of arms and legs
    looked blue in the water,
        while she wheezed and coughed

and the red rubber duck
    bobbled about by itself,
        ignored.

And the tub in the gray Victorian heap
    on Oak Street (Trucksville, 1951),
        where once each day for ten whole minutes

Mark could relax,
    relieved of the steel
        stiff-knee leg braces,

kneel and crawl,
    splash with the same old
        red rubber duck.

    vii
And the bathtub of hand-hewn onyx
    installed by Enzo Falorio
        in the old Ruffer mansion

on Talisman Road
    (Hunting Valley, Ohio, 1966)
        Of course we remember with glee:

it cost, they said, some
    thirty-five thousand dollars.
        As guests, we bathed in liquid ebony,

afterward
    saying to Grandmother Lillie May:
        Now there's conspicuous consumption for you!

only to have her observe
    (ever practical, ever fair):
        Think of the work it gave the hewers of onyx.

    viii

O many and various bathtubs,
    reminders of onyx and cockroach,
        of lizards and jacaranda,

waterfalls, bloodstreams, one red rubber duck,
    bodies of lovers and children,
        washings away of soil and sorrow,

O bathtubs we remember,
    are you still there?
        Who bathes in you now

in Emigrant Gap, Montclair, Coamo Springs,
    in London, Shavertown, Trucksville,
        New York, Hunting Valley?

Where is the water that laved us,
    soothed and cleansed us,
        warmed and pleasured us?

Surely high alpine snow drifts,
    mineral springs,
        Thames and Lake Erie

accepted its coming at first
    with purest intentions,
        while elsewhere

(and somewhat less surely)
    vast sewage disposal systems
        went through their arcane motions

trying to circulate
    purified lifestreams
        throughout the world's body.

Perhaps a Mojave aquifer
    holds your dischargings,
        O bathtubs,

or perhaps they still circle the planet
    falling at random (wherever
        random might be),

as for instance a tough Sherpa guide
    might wipe from his smooth copper chin
        snowflakes that once,

a lifetime ago,
    moistened a kiss
        in a honeymoon bathtub.

How You Got the Two-Inch-Thick Twelve-Inch-in-Diameter Piece of Corning Glass for Your Schmidt Camera Telescope

When Pearlie laced their scrambled eggs with rat poison, the Millers survived, though Great-uncle George was so upset he fired Pearlie. Mrs. Isinger, P.N., who catered to Great-aunt Minnie's every whim, was horrified and wondered what the world was coming to. Minnie's brother, Ozzie, brought a "comfort gift" of brand new clothespins in a canvas bag, forgetting that last Christmas he had given Minnie one just like it, together with a handsome monkey wrench.

> The day we met and knew that we would marry, you named me Juli.

Each June a hired ambulance transported Minnie, George and Mrs. I. to a rented house in Ocean Grove, New Jersey. With them in a separate car went Yourydice, successor to Pearlie, with the necessaries for Minnie's comfort. Windows were closed, curtains drawn, Minnie ensconced in the second floor best bed, and the Millers spent the summer at the shore. Nor sea, nor sand, nor sky was seen, nor ocean breeze admitted. On September 1st the Millers returned en masse to Littleton.

> You must have wondered why you never met a single member of my mother's family.

After George died Minnie changed her ways, arose from her bed, got dressed and was driven by Lillie Mae, my mother, to the "Cadillac Shore." She pointed to a car, said "I'll take that one," pulled a fistful of cash from the pocket of her old fur coat, and paid full price, no questions asked. Lillie Mae drove her home in it. Shopping daily for the household, Cousin Patience, Minnie's

niece, would top her list with: Number One—go out and start
the car.

So I told you why on our wedding night in 1938. Who'd want
to marry a looney bin? Later you asked me what I'd say in my
thank-you note to Great-aunt Minnie for her wedding gift
of seventy-five dollars. Easy, I said, we used it to buy the very
first glassware we could find.

Ecology Note—Spring, 1985

There are four
dusky seaside sparrows
left in the world,
all of them male.

Small gray widowers,
they hop busily
from pole to pole
in a Florida zoo,

pipe cheerful mating songs,
then settle, poised,
gray heads atilt,
to listen

for the answering calls.

Sonnet at Seventy

O but there should be some new kind of voice
to tell my love, to tell my love for you—
another speech, tongue, idiom, fresh choice
of sound and accent, some more subtle hue
of phrase and tone, a newer instrument
on which this newest music may be played:
all the old expressions have been spent
on the old meanings, everything has been said.
Yet does it matter how the word is spoken,
so it is spoken? The simple voice of love
takes whatever form may best betoken
the ancient tale it is new telling of,
a serenade, or hieroglyphics—and
I love you chalked on fence by grubby hand.

Some Pig

Your pig aorta has sprung a leak. Some pig,
who died eleven years ago last October
to give you a piece of his heart, other things being equal
might have enjoyed eleven more years of life
before a valve started to leak in his porcine chest—
though other things being equal he would more likely
long since have been slaughtered for bacon, which, by the way,
you wouldn't eat for some time, because, you said,
it would make you feel cannibalistic.
I never gave much thought, before, to that pig,
just took his aorta for granted.
Now I think about him and his life and you and your life,
the lives of pigs and men and how
maybe, one of these days, some other pig.

The Noon News—January 1991

Shall we have lunch and take a look at the war?
Or would you prefer to sit at the kitchen table and decide
if there's enough sand to de-ice the duckboards
(not how desert sand is damaging bombers),
whom to call if the oil tank in the barn is leaking
(not that today they're assessing the number of tank kills)?

We could pretend the whole thing's a video game,
and if we turn off the TV the bombs will implode
in one silent slow diminishing speck of light,
instead of blossoming over an ancient city
where the Thief of Baghdad sits cherishing mad dreams—
but this morning they said the results of bomb damage assessment
were inconclusive, except, of course,
for Lt. Cmdr. Michael S. Speicher, of Jacksonville, Florida,
whose distinction it is to be named the first
American combat casualty,
something his family can always remember.

                                        Come on,
let's take our lunch trays into the living room now
and watch the war.

Evening, January 1991

We're sitting now in our comfortable orange chairs.
There's a glow from a couple of logs in the cast iron stove
—a Vermont Defiant—on the other side of the room.
On the other side of the world it's 3:00 a.m.
and over the desert bombs are bursting in air.
We know this is so: the picture is very clear
on the TV screen. We see the quiet flares
while the commentator speaks in a mildly grave,
almost indifferent tone, as if war
is something that happens between commercials. We
are, respectively, eighty-five and seventy-four,
so we're coming down the other side of the hill
and occasionally wonder what the end will be.
If we were to fall asleep in our orange chairs
with the embers gleaming still in the cast iron stove,
and fail to wake in the morning, could it be said
we were lucky to have died by friendly fire?

Parkinson's

God damn it to hell, *move*—God damn it, I say move, get the hell—
oh for God's sake *do* something—I can't hold—shit—it's not a solo
dance, dammit, move your right foot, *move* it for God's sake, move
it, OK, now move your left foot—that's right, I mean left—hell's bells—
now move your right foot—*good*—an inch, you got an inch—now move
your left foot—you're *sinking* straight down on your spine, you fool,
all one-hundred-and-seventy-five fucking pounds of you, stupid, shove
your Goddamned right foot—an inch—just a stinking inch that's all I'm
asking, one measly shitty inch—*good*—now the left—OK you did it, do
it again now with your right—*keep going* till I can hook my ankle around
the leg of the chair and pull it toward me—good (*ah God he's slipping*—
No!) foot! foot! I never want to hear that word again move it I say
may God damn you to everlasting hell if you don't move it
now! now!

ok. sit down. we made it. o, my dear, my very dear, we made it.

Ode

O brain
feathermost part of me
lightsome mind–light
light sum of thoughts
(oughts?)
addled
coddled
(odd, some
body's
body
battled it into being, bringing it forth)
bat-like
clinging in darkness
cavern of soul
winging alone at night
from its hole
in soundless search of a whole in the void
avoiding all truth
evading touch

O brain
weathermost part of me
blown
dust devil
the vane must rust
whatever the wind
henceforth
all points are north

Let's see

how blind will I be?
One-eye
two-eye
three-eye blind?
What about the mind's eye
Wordsworth mentions?
What about hindsight
insight
foresight?
What about tears?

Can I use the eyes in the back of my head
after all these years?

What about dreams
and remembrance of color,
and faces—what about faces
when they begin to disappear?
What about fear?
While the doors of the rooms in my head
are slowly closing,
what about dread?
And then at last, when push comes to shove,
what about love?

What if

I took my heavy-hearted heavy-footed
courage in my hands and lifted
all those ugly chunks of
procrastination holding down
the piles and piles of papers
heaped on every horizontal surface
in the three rooms I'm learning to call
home

        and

stuffed some clothes a toothbrush and
a handful of assorted pills red
white pink purple into a
duffle bag I'll have to go out
and buy tomorrow because I must have
sold all my luggage to
the mover

        and

set off next Sunday morning
to drive two-and-a-half hours
of highway south to visit yes
that's it visit what was my
home.

Would they know me?
Am I who I used to be?

I'd better call first.

Meditations on a Broomstick

Think I'll try one.
Often wondered if I could fly one.
Must be nice,
to be up and off and away in a trice,
nobody watching but owls and mice
and one black cat.

Tall black hat,
long black cloak blowing out behind
in a long black wind.

Here we go...
Ahhhh...

Look below:
town is a patch of winking lights.
Tonight is the darkest night of nights,
and one of the coldest too.
Heigh-ho,
for a witch's eye view
of the wide wide world is one of the sights
reserved for the few,
the very few
who are willing to try one.

Chilling
      to
          fly
         one!
Ahhhh!
But fun!
Fun!

Odd:
I never thought before
a broom might have another use than sweeping

a kitchen floor and a pantry floor.
Stood behind the door
twenty years and more—
twenty years of doing and sweeping,
twenty years of waking and sleeping,
promise-keeping.

Now when tomorrow's dawn comes creeping
and I'm not there,
doors will open and shut and voices will call
from room to empty room.
And one will say:
She's gone and so's her broom.
She's gone away.
She's probably gone to stay.

And silence will fall.

But they won't know where.

Night Voices

i
The Gargoyles

We mark the hours.
Mute, we leer from the foot of her bed.
Night long our silent clamor deafens her.
Wakeful, she listens as one by one
old lies drip from our tongueless mouths.

ii
The Nightmares

We are her dreams.
We graze in the fields of her sleep,
nibbling at stalks of long-branched, thorny cares,
or race in a velvet stillness,
our great hooves pounding terror into her brain.

iii
The Worryworts

Poisonous, ugly weeds,
we grow in the hoofprints of her nightmares,
blossom in manure-rich soil.
She cannot uproot us. No charm by daylight
will make us vanish. Once sprouted, we flourish.

Geriatric Ward, St. Vincent Hospital

There were four of us—the others,
one a feisty little Irish lady whose visiting family daily
overflowed her space, one who was very quiet, lying
with her face to the wall, and one who kept mumbling
to herself all the time. It was dull,
with nothing to see but green walls and a window
looking out on another part of the building, but
when I woke the first morning I heard
the faint tinkling of a bell from down the corridor
and a kind of brushing sound, then in swept a big man
wearing a cassock and he went up to the Irish lady and said
good morning how are you feeling the body of Christ
then swooped around the curtain to the quiet one and said
good morning how are you feeling the body of Christ
started toward me, checked, nodded,
passed on to the mumbling one and said
good morning how are you feeling the body of Christ
then swept out the door and I lay there for a long time
wondering just how
those old women were feeling the body of Christ

Leaf Burning

Soon I must gather
The leaves of a year,
Heap them together here.

Time and the weather,
A merciless pair,
Having had their way with them,
See how they fare
When I with a barrow
And rake have my say with them.

Each leafy feather
A feathery leaf—
All taken together
Piled in the barrow
Will be lighter than sorrow
In weight and in color—
Gray is for grief,
These are still mellow
Dark honey-yellow,
Though getting duller.

Now if tomorrow
Be windless and clear,
Here by the road
I'll come with my barrow
And load upon load
Turn out in the gutter.
Leaf unto flame,
As lover to lover,
Will leap to discover
More of the utter
Abandon of living
Now in their dying

Than ever they showed
Before they were shaken
Loose from their stems,
Unless I'm mistaken.

Light wind

and fog, lifting
with a dripping brush
on paper-thin blur of sky
dirty flecks of black wings over
a drag of tattered branches dipping

pale
a wash of watercolor weather

light wind, dry
blow dry blow high
blow lemon-light the whole dull low
gray green-sea-water sky

fog, drifting
with a dripping
brush
a wash
of light
wind, lifting

The Voices of Things

When I stir with a special spoon in a certain bowl,
the spoon says *Irene Irene*, and I think of Irene,
her flowing hair, black eyes, her dance of death.

When the windshield-wipers prophesy my doom,
hinting *victim victim victim* through the rain,
I see the wall of granite I barely missed.

And the door of the attic, closing, whispers *Wait*
while I stand at the top of the stairwell looking down
over the spiraled railing into a pit.

Even when they are mute I seem to hear
voices of things in murmurous suggestion,
as if I were being asked to enter their world,

perhaps, in time, to become a thing myself.

1. People don't pass away

they die.
Let me tell you right here and now:
I'm never going to pass away. I'm
going to die. Why
are so many people fearful of saying
that neat little three-letter word?
And let me tell you something else: if
when I die anyone speaks of my passing away
I'll pass right back and haunt him.

Passing away!
I can see me now: my spirit-self ascending
released at last from its habitat bag of bones,
hovering, faint pencil outline, drifting
farther and farther into the sky and fading
shin by thigh by hip by elbow.
                                        My beloved,
did you "pass away" on that April night in the hospice bed,
up through the ceiling into the Little Bill Room, then the roof?
or did you do your passing sideways through the living room
by the fireplace and the blue chair and the seven shelves of books?
out through the mudroom over the waterhog doormat
through the screen and down the wheelchair ramp
to take off in your striped pajamas, soaring
over the field across the driveway?
                                        Passing away, indeed.
Not you. You went to sleep, dark-rimmed glasses in place,
the little headset radio's yellow speakers
clapped to your ears—
and sometime during the night you died.
It was as simple as that.
I know. I was there.

2. On second thought

I like to think of you floating
into the mudroom and over the waterhog doormat
and down the wheelchair ramp to take off
—remember the silver balloon
our neighbor tied to a fence post
to honor our fifty years together?
how we took it to the center of that field
each holding a strand of paper ribbon,
looked at each other, grinned
and set it free?
how it dodged a tree and went sparkling in sunlight,
twirled and danced eastward higher and higher,
diminishing into a brilliant dot
and then vanished? and how I said it would land
in Framingham, and how you, O man of vision,
predicted Portugal?

Your Ashes

I've scattered them in the south field,
among those tiny star-shaped flowers
that each spring gleam like miniature constellations
in an upside-down green sky.

Ladder #13

Made of touchwood, amadou,
tinder prepared from fungus,
spongy, giving

Like a beanstalk:
swaying, leaf-runged,
not to be trusted for the long climb

Never walk under one
slanted against a building
unless you carry the black cat,

Familiar of Hel,
goddess of those who die of old age

Touch wood

Redbird

The sudden gust of wind
that shakes the oak
sends like a puff of somber smoke
a flurry of dark red leaves out over the road.

One leaf however has wings,
and now from a low pine bough defying the wind,
he sings.

About the Author

JULI (ELIZABETH) NUNLISt was born in 1916. Multifaceted, she has been a musician, composer, and poet. In her career, she has taught music to dancers, choreographers and dance teachers. She writes: "As long as I can remember I've tried to write both poetry and music." She studied at Randolph-Macon's Woman's College and graduated magna cum laude, Phi Beta Kappa, from Barnard College in 1940. In 1957, at age 40, she entered Manhattan School of Music, where she received both Bachelor and Master's of Music degrees. She has composed chamber music, a one-act opera, orchestral and choral pieces, as well as many songs, in three languages.

She was on the faculty of Hathaway Brown School where she taught writing and became chairman of the Fine Arts Department. She attended the Radcliffe Poetry Seminars and The Frost Place Poetry Festival, and she started The Princeton Writer's Workshop. Her poems have been published in such journals as: *Field, The Christian Science Monitor, Beloit Poetry Journal,* and *Appalachia.*

Juli currently resides in Lebanon, New Hampshire.